OWJC
OCT 05

Pebble™ Plus

A Visit to

The Apple Orchard

by Patricia J. Murphy

Consulting Editor: Gail Saunders-Smith, PhD
Reading Consultant: Jennifer Norford, Senior Consultant
Mid-continent Research for Education and Learning
Aurora, Colorado

Capstone press

Mankato, Minnesota

Pebble Plus is published by Capstone Press
151 Good Counsel Drive, P.O. Box 669, Mankato, Minnesota 56002
www.capstonepress.com

1 2 3 4 5 6 09 08 07 06 05 04

Library of Congress Cataloging-in-Publication Data
Murphy, Patricia J., 1963–
    The apple orchard/by Patricia J. Murphy.
    p. cm.—(Pebble plus: A visit to)
    Includes bibliographical references and index.
    ISBN 0-7368-2579-7 (hardcover)
    1. Apples—Juvenile literature. 2. Orchards—Juvenile literature. [1. Apples. 2. Orchards.] I. Title.
II. Series: A visit to (Mankato, Minn.)
SB363.M87 2005
634'.11—dc22   2003024959

Summary: Simple text and photos present a visit to an apple orchard.

Editorial Credits
Sarah L. Schuette, editor; Enoch Peterson, book designer; Jennifer Bergstrom, series designer;
    Karen Hieb, product planning editor

Photo Credits
Capstone Press/Gary Sundermeyer, all

The author thanks Bob Quig at Quig's Apple Orchard, in Mundelein, Illionis, and Michael Berst of the Apple
Journal for research assistance. She dedicates this book to Erik and Olivia.

Capstone Press thanks Topper and the staff of Sponsel's Minnesota Harvest Orchard in Jordan, Minnesota, and
Welsh Heritage Farms in Lake Crystal, Minnesota, for assistance with photo shoots.

Note to Parents and Teachers

The series A Visit to supports national social studies standards related to the production,
distribution, and consumption of goods and services. This book describes and illustrates
a visit to an apple orchard. The images support early readers in understanding the text.
The repetition of words and phrases helps early readers learn new words. This book also
introduces early readers to subject-specific vocabulary words, which are defined in the
Glossary section. Early readers may need assistance to read some words and to use
the Table of Contents, Glossary, Read More, Internet Sites, and Index/Word List sections
of the book.

Word Count: 114
Early-Intervention Level: 11

Table of Contents

The Apple Orchard

Apples grow in apple orchards. An apple orchard is a tasty place to visit.

Rows of apple trees grow
in orchards. Different kinds
of apples grow on different
kinds of apple trees.

Picking Apples

Workers pick apples in fall.

They put apples into bags.

Workers drive tractors.

The tractors pull wagons

filled with apples.

11

Machines wash and
polish apples. The apples
move along belts in
a packing line.

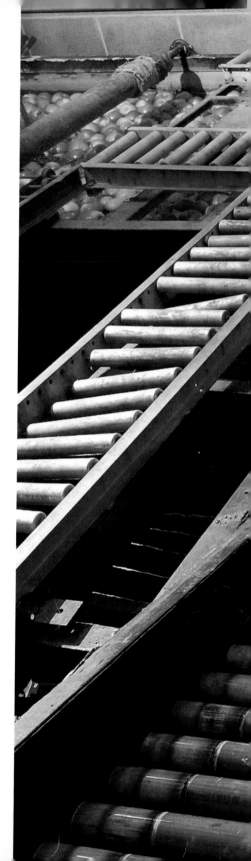

13

Machines sort apples
by size. Workers pack
apples into crates.

Eating Apples

Visitors can taste different
kinds of apples.

PONSELLI   CONNELL RED   CORTLAND   MCINTOSH

Visitors shop at the apple store. They buy bags of apples, apple pies, cider, and other items.

HONEYGOLD
$4.50/ 3 LB BAG
$7.50/ 5 LB BAG

CORTLAND
$3.00/ 3 LB BAG
$5.00/ 5 LB BAG

W. GREENING

Apple orchards grow healthy snacks. An apple orchard is a fun place to visit.

Glossary

cider—a beverage made by pressing apples

crate—a large wooden box

orchard—a field or farm where fruit trees grow

polish—to rub to make shiny

sort—to arrange in a group; apples are sorted by size and color.

tractor—a heavy machine that is used to pull machinery and other heavy loads

wagon—a vehicle with wheels that is used to carry heavy loads

Read More

Mayr, Diane. *Out and About at the Apple Orchard.* Field Trips. Minneapolis: Picture Window Books, 2003.

Taus-Bolstad, Stacy. *From Shoot to Apple.* Start to Finish. Minneapolis: Lerner, 2003.

Wolfman, Judy. *Life on an Apple Orchard.* Life on a Farm. Minneapolis: Carolrhoda, 2004.

Internet Sites

FactHound offers a safe, fun way to find Internet sites related to this book. All of the sites on FactHound have been researched by our staff.

Here's how:

1. Visit *www.facthound.com*

2. Type in this special code **0736825797** for age-appropriate sites. Or enter a search word related to this book for a more general search.

3. Click on the **Fetch It** button.

FactHound will fetch the best sites for you!

Index/Word List